Simpler Times

THOMAS KINKADE

with Anne Christian Buchanan

HARVEST HOUSE PUBLISHERS
Eugene, Oregon 97402

SIMPLER TIMES

Copyright © 1996 by Thomas Kinkade, Media Arts Group, Inc.
Published by Harvest House Publishers
Eugene, Oregon 97402

Library of Congress Cataloging-in-Publication Data

Kinkade, Thomas, 1958-
   Simpler Times / Thomas Kinkade with Anne Christian Buchanan.
       p.   cm.
   ISBN 1-56507-416-5 (alk. paper)
    1. Peace of mind.   2. Simplicity   3. Life.   4. Quality of Life.
   I. Buchanan, Anne Christian.   II. Title.
   BF637.P3K55   1996
   179'.9–dc20   96-6397
                                                                          CIP

   Media Arts Group, Inc.
   10 Almaden Blvd., 9th Floor
   San Jose, CA 95113
   1.800.366.3733

Printed in the United States of America.

Design and production by:
Koechel Peterson & Associates
Minneapolis, Minnesota

96 97 98 99 00 01 02 03 04 05 // 10 9 8 7 6 5 4 3 2 1

To my wife

and children,

who share all of

my simpler times.

Contents

A Picture of Simplicity

It is the simple things of life that make living worthwhile, the sweet fundamental things such as love and duty, work and rest and living close to nature.

—LAURA INGALLS WILDER

I hear the yearning almost every day from people who talk or write to me about my paintings. "That's where I want to be," they say of a scene I've depicted. "I want to step into that painting, walk down that path, and live in that house with the glowing windows."

Obviously, they don't really want to live in a painting. They are simply desiring the world of peace and simplicity I try to portray in my work. They are yearning for a life that focuses on what is truly important and what is truly beautiful—a life that is different from the rushed, cluttered existence our popular culture promotes.

There is nothing wrong with that kind of yearning. It's my yearning, too, and the reason I paint the kind of scenes I do. In fact, I believe something has gone seriously wrong if we don't have that kind of hunger for a better, simpler way of life. Human beings were not made for the rush-hour, freeway kind of life we try so frantically to live. We were made for calm, not chaos, and that is why we long for simpler times. Somewhere deep inside we know that simpler times are better times.

That's the kind of life I strive to evoke in my paintings. It's the kind of life I'm committed to building for myself and my family.

And it's the foundational message I want to share with the world through my work and through my life.

A Separate Peace

Choosing Simplicity in a Complex Age

Life is measured by the number of things you are alive to.

— MALTBIE D. BABCOCK

A separate peace.

It has happened in history for a variety of reasons, honorable and dishonorable. Many countries have enthusiastically gone to war. Banners flying, boots shining, a proud little nation joins the mighty alliance and marches off to war. Eager to defend its honor, it plunges enthusiastically into the fray.

Years later, the banners have grown ragged, and the little nation that marched off so proudly has begun to wonder if the war is really worth it. Perhaps it's time for a separate peace.

Does that scenario sound familiar?

To me, it conjures up images of a lot of people I know. They are weary and discouraged just from trying to keep up with the wars they thought they wanted— the war to get ahead, the war to keep up with others, the war for bigger and better and more and more. It's a battleground offered each day in the modern world.

If you don't believe me, just picture the freeway closest to where you live. Or the mall on sale day. Your local McDonald's at lunch hour. A sales meeting in a nearby office.

As far as I can see, "normal" life as we know it in the latter part of the twentieth century is not normal at all. It's not designed to make human life happier or more meaningful or even more productive.

And without even knowing it, perhaps even without wanting to, you find yourself hurling into the fray, without really considering whether you have an option.

But you do.

You may not be able to shut down the war, but you don't have to fight somebody else's battles. You don't have to surrender your sanity to someone else's insanity.

You can choose to make a separate peace.

On a little or large level, you can make choices that take you away from the battleground. In the process, you will be choosing to live in saner, simpler times.

How do you do it? At the very simplest level, you find a place to retreat. You arrange for a refuge where

you can rest and be renewed before returning to the fray. Your corner of peace may be as simple as a comfortable chair with an old-fashioned lamp beside it. You turn on the lamp and sink into the chair in the circle of warm light. Or your peaceful place can be a book; you turn the pages and step through the word windows into another world. It can be a painting—a painting that pulls you into its vision of beauty, that gives you a picture of what a peaceful world can be.

A special room in my studio offers me one of my favorite retreats. It is lined with books by and about my heroes—the artists who feed my spirit and enlarge my horizons. I love to sit in the chair by the window and pore over the beautifully printed monographs, losing myself in the works of the greatest painters who have ever lived. They inspire me, they challenge me, they open up new worlds for me. They also offer me peace.

Another favorite retreat for me is a lawn chair in the small grassy yard outside my studio. In that chair I have perfected the art of taking mini-vacations. Even on my most hectic days I can manage to take fifteen minutes to enjoy a sandwich or pray or doze in the sun—just closing my eyes and drifting.

My own work is a retreat for me as well. I live in my paintings as I work on them, and I deliberately paint scenes that serve as places of refuge for battle-weary people. When I am painting a scene, I am walking down the path, peering around

the curve of the river, wondering what's around the bend. I am crossing the bridge, strolling in the sun-dappled shadows, feeling the peace. I have even been known to shiver on a warm summer day while painting a snowy winter scene.

Your place of retreat, your little corner of peace, may be very different from mine. The specifics don't really matter. The point is you find a place or an activity that gives your senses a chance to unwind and lets you catch a fresh vision of peacetime possibilities. Furnish it comfortably. Make it beautiful. Use it often.

But if a little corner of peace makes such a difference, doesn't it make sense to make larger life choices with an eye to simplicity and peace? Of course it does.

Ever since my wife, Nanette, and I met at age thirteen, we have had a dream of creating a home together —a haven where we could live and raise our children. As our lives have moved forward, we have fought to hold on to that peaceful vision. Its details have changed, but not its central character. Again and again we have tried to make choices that would help us forge our separate peace.

For instance, we've taken every opportunity to avoid spending sizable chunks of our lives simply moving from one place to another. Our current home was chosen with exactly that vision in mind. Our house was built in an earlier era and is located an easy walk or bike ride away from the village center. That village is where we shop and go on dates together and take our kids to school. Whenever we can, we walk or ride bikes to do our errands, turning necessary chores into family outings. And we've managed to all but eliminate a commute to work. When the opportunity came, we purchased the cottage next door and converted it into a studio. That decision grants daily rewards as I make my thirty-second commute through the redwoods, as Nanette comes over to stretch canvases and talk, as my daughters crash through the door after school to share their latest news.

Another battle we have chosen to opt out of is the information revolution. We don't surf the Net. We don't follow CNN. In fact, we've chosen to keep television out of our house entirely. This is not because we are opposed to the medium of television, but because we are opposed to what television tends to do in our lives. In our experience, television is a thief that robs us of our time together and steals our peace.

When we are watching TV, we are not riding our bikes or playing in the yard or having couch-pillow fights with our girls in the living room. Instead, we are soaking up the subtle and not-so-subtle messages that we should want more, more, more . . . and sacrifice our peace if necessary to obtain it.

In fact, saying no to the messages of our surrounding culture is a peace-choice I try to make almost every day. The word *no* has become a real lifesaver to me, and I use it without guilt. More often than not, in my experience, using the word *yes* in response to the world around me generates a harvest of chaos. The word *no*, on the other hand, generates a great harvest of peace in our lives.

For example, I have learned to say no to commitments that steal away our family time and eat into my painting time. I find myself practicing that word *no* on a daily basis:

I went to the woods because I wished to live deliberately, to front only the essential facts of life, and see if I could not learn what it had to teach, and not, when I came to die, discover that I had not lived. I did not wish to live what was not life, living is so dear.

— HENRY DAVID THOREAU

"No, I can't have visitors today."

"No, I can't attend that meeting. I spend my evenings with my family."

"No, I can't grant that interview. I need to paint today."

And of course, I need to say no to myself as well, at times.

No isn't always an easy or comfortable choice. Most of us are so accustomed to overstimulation that peace feels strange to us; it makes us nervous. Simplicity can be an acquired taste, especially in a society that revels in complexity.

But what an improvement when we finally begin to feel at home with a simpler way of life. What a sense of empowerment when we realize we can say no to the constant bombardment of our minds and senses. What a surge of energy when we realize that saying no is really a way of saying yes to all we really care about.

I want to say yes, for example, to deep and intimate relationships. And I would far rather invest my energy in maintaining a vital marriage and raising well-loved children than in getting ahead and creating an empire. I believe that how I treat my family, how I spend my time with them, has eternal implications. So I want to feel assured that I am influencing their life for the better. I want to teach them, tickle them, discipline them, hug them. I want to know what they're reading, what they're learning, what they're wondering about.

I am willing to say no to a lot of things—to say yes to my family in that way.

I also want to say yes to experiences, to surprise, to serendipity—all the things that have no room to happen if I'm saying yes to all the demands of the world around me. I want to experience my life rather than spend it on the treadmill with the rest of the rat race. And that, too, means I have to say no to a lot of good things that take my time. It means I must give up some opportunities, take off the get-ahead blinders, make space in my life for experience to happen.

Yes, I make plans. Yes, I have goals. But stopping to examine a bug with my five-year-old may well reap more long-term rewards than beating a deadline.

I also want to say a deep, enthusiastic yes to the work that I am called to do in this world. It's a harmful fallacy that work has to be a source of stress and anxiety and striving and that "getting away from it all" has to mean leaving work behind. But saying yes to my work doesn't mean doing everything I am asked to do or even everything I want to do.

My personal calling at this time of my life, in addition to being an active, caring, involved husband and father, is to create paintings and books that reach out and bless the lives of others. Everything else is peripheral—even important tasks, even things I enjoy or that get me excited.

When I learn to say a deep, passionate yes to the things that really matter—and no to whatever gets in the way of that yes—then the peace begins to settle onto my life like golden sunlight sifting to a forest floor.

And that, I find, is a peace worth fighting for.

Time is but the stream

I go a-fishing in. I drink at it;

but while I drink I see

the sandy bottom and

detect how shallow it is.

Its thin current slides away,

but eternity remains.

I would drink deeper;

fish in the sky, whose bottom

is pebbly with stars. . . .

—HENRY DAVID THOREAU

A True View

The Fine Art of Keeping Perspective

Let the form of an object be what it may —

light, shade, and perspective will always make it beautiful.

— JOHN CONSTABLE

I t's true in painting, and it's true in life: How things look depends on the way you see them. And both a well-received painting and a fulfilling life depend upon keeping a true perspective.

I worked recently on a painting that challenged and inspired me. It is a view of the Golden Gate bridge, depicted from across the bay. In the foreground, gentle waves curl. The beautiful bridge curves gracefully into the distance over the surging waters of the bay, with the sparkling city beyond.

It's a beautiful scene. It took my breath when I first looked at the bridge from that particular angle. And my ability to paint it depended on how I managed the complex perspective required. The waves in the foreground needed to appear larger than those next to the bridge. The relative distance between the girders needed to be just right to convince the eye of the shape and curve of the bridge. The water in between needed to sparkle and draw the eye toward the bridge, which is the focus

of the painting, and on to the distant city. To pull that painting off, I needed to look with an alert, unprejudiced eye and then employ all my energy and artistic skill to reproduce what my artistic eye saw.

In art, perspective is both a viewpoint and a technique. Perspective is the lens and angle from which the painter views the world of the painting, and it is also a set of skills that enable the artist to paint that world believably.

When I reproduce those perceptions on canvas, I am able to create a landscape that seems three-dimensional and real. With perspective, I can bring the painting to life.

Perspective also allows me to shape the reality of a painting, to change the world subtly, to achieve my goals as an artist. I can emphasize certain elements, minimize others, even add or subtract items, using my perspective skills to work these elements into a believable and, I hope, beautiful whole.

And yes, all this applies to perspective in life as well as in painting. Our perspective or viewpoint involves the way we look at life. But our perspective also shapes our living.

If I am looking at life through a perspective of gratitude and hope, for instance, I will live and think differently than if my view was one of bitterness and anger. The same is true of the way I look at myself. If I maintain a balanced perspective on me—honestly recognizing my flaws and shortcomings, honestly appreciating my gifts and talents—I will live accordingly, and this balanced view will shape my life.

This is not to say that any perspective is just as good as any other. The modern assumption in both art and life is that perspective is relative, that one view is just as good as another. But I don't buy that. Although there are a variety of possible perspectives in any life, I believe there really is a true view that best conforms to the way the world is designed. In my life, a true perspective helps me keep my priorities straight. The big things in my life—my family, my work, my faith in God—stay big, and receive most of my energy. The little things receive less attention. I am able to laugh at myself and my problems, to find contentment in my present circumstances, and to maintain hope for the future.

In my experience, however, perspective is prone to slippage. When I am working too hard, when I let my ambition get the best of me or allow my schedule to be overloaded, my perspective easily becomes skewed. When I'm not getting enough sleep or eating right or keeping my spiritual life in tune,

It is only with the heart
that one can see rightly;
what is essential is
invisible to the eye.
– ANTOINE DE SAINT-EXUPÉRY

my perspective can get warped. I lose touch with who I really am and with what is important in my life. And those are the times when I begin majoring on minors, sweating the small stuff, taking my frustrations out on others. Those are the times when my daily tasks seem difficult, the people in my life seem unreasonable, when I take myself entirely too seriously.

Fortunately, I usually know what to do to get my perspective back in line. I have quite a collection of artist's tools that help me keep the perspective true in my paintings. And I have discovered some perspective-preserving techniques that help in my life as well.

Quiet time and solitude are vital to helping me keep perspective. I consider myself incredibly fortunate to have so much quiet built into my profession. I spend long hours by myself at my easel. And while I work, I think—of the future, of my loved ones, of God's goodness and the many exciting opportunities that surround me. I ponder the challenges I face, the needs of others, the direction my life is going.

As my thoughts unfold, forming and reforming to the rhythm of my brushwork, something else often happens as well. Quietly, almost unnoticeably, the wisdom and guidance of God will begin to settle on my active mind like gently falling snow on a busy street. That's why I like to think of these moments of quiet reflection as a form of prayer. Because they open up my mind and spirit to God's presence, they are doubly important in helping me keep my perspective true.

As vital as quiet time is, however, I find it hard to maintain a balanced perspective without input from other people and a chance to bounce my ideas off friends and colleagues. So I read. I listen to tapes. I seek out friends for discussions. Most important, I talk to my wife, Nanette.

Until I married Nanette, I was an inveterate journaler. I wrote down all my thoughts and observations and feelings, and the act of writing helped me keep my life in perspective. Now, I like to think of Nanette as my journal, because I tell her everything, and our discussions help us both get a better handle on our situations. After so many years together, I feel I haven't really experienced something until I've shared it with her.

When we talk and pray together, my off-center focus gradually shifts, and my world comes into focus again.

Our talks are not all deadly serious, though. Nanette and I laugh together a lot. Sometimes we end up holding our sides and stomping the floor, laughing so hard we can't catch our breath.

One of the things we laugh about is my sometimes feeble attempts to maintain a "macho image." Maybe it comes from not wanting to be typecast as a "sensitive artist." Maybe I just like playing the role a bit. But there is a part of me that likes leather jackets and fly fishing and huge motorcycles—you know, all the "manly" stuff. And I can almost pull off the Ernest Hemingway routine until something hilarious happens to poke a hole in my pretensions—like riding through town on my

loud motorcycle only to realize I've got a dab of green paint on my nose! It's hard to take yourself too seriously in predicaments like that.

Most important of all, I maintain my perspective by trying to take the long view, the wider view. I try to step back from my life and get a vision for how things fit together. I try to determine what is temporal and what is timeless.

And I count my blessings.

I take the old, corny, totally dependable route of listing all the things I have to be thankful for. My art. My family. The fact that I woke up this morning and was able to walk and talk and breathe. The fact that in the day to come I will have another chance to get my perspective adjusted and see my life for what it is. Truly blessed.

The essence of the true view is that each of us is blessed beyond what we could ask or think, if we just take the time to realize it. Each of us can thank God for the indescribable gift that is life. To be living is to be handed a precious white canvas upon which each of us can create a painting of great depth and meaning. A painting that can be full of joy and peace. The beautiful painting of our lives.

Each life is a masterpiece in the making. And if your perspective is true, the whole canvas will be beautiful.

The real voyage

of discovery

consists not in

seeking new landscapes

but in having

new eyes.

– Marcel Proust

The Warmth from the Windows

Welcoming Yourself into Your Own Life

Thus, simply as a little child,

we learn a home is made from love.

Warm as the golden hearthfire on the floor.

—AUTHOR UNKNOWN

Someone asked me once why I paint so many houses and cottages with warm, glowing windows. At first I didn't know what to say. After all, how does an artist explain why he paints what he does?

I've thought a lot about that question, though, and now I think I have an answer. I paint glowing windows because glowing windows say home to me. Glowing windows say welcome. They say all is well. They say that someone's waiting, someone cares enough to turn a light on.

For a person like me, who grew up in a single-parent household and often had to come home to an empty house, that "someone's home" glow is irresistible. It draws the eye like a brightly wrapped present, a promise of wonderful secrets inside. Can you see a brightly lit window without even the smallest urge to go peek in, to see what the people are doing and what their lives are like? I can't either.

In fact, as I am dabbing brushfuls of golden paint on those windows—whether on a rambling Victorian mansion or a tiny little fishing cabin—I am always imagining a world of family gatherings, of quiet times spent in the company of loved ones.

I can almost smell the toasty aromas of popcorn or a pie baking. I can hear the lively sounds of laughter and perhaps the tinkle of a music box. I can feel the plush and silky textures of a velvet settee and a baby's cheek. And I see it all lit by the golden glow of a fireplace or a candle or a lamp with a fringed shade.

I paint warm windows, in other words, because I envision a perpetual warm reunion.

I have that same feeling every night when I leave my studio. I love to close my studio door

and make my way across the small lawn, up the stone steps, across the patio to our kitchen door.

Outside, all is dark. But through the glowing kitchen window I can see Nanette moving back and forth, singing gently as she adds the last touches to our dinner. And I can imagine what else is going on inside.

Seven-year-old Merritt is lifting the lid to the pot of soup and stirring while she tells her mother about her new pet snail. (It's in a jar by the door, waiting for me to see.) Five-year-old Chandler is perched on a stool, "helping," determined to do whatever her big sister does. Baby Winsor in her highchair is grinning her two-toothed grin through a mouthful of sweet potatoes.

And around it all there is the warm glow of anticipation.

I'm on my way home. And I know what will happen next. The girls will race to the door to grab my knees and jump in my arms and show me their snail. Nanette will give me a kiss. Winsor will grin and blow bubbles.

We'll eat. And then we'll play. And then we'll read together and bundle the children off to bed after listening to their goodnight prayers. There will be time for Nanette and me to sit and talk awhile.

This is my home, my welcoming world. This is my anchor, the resting place for my heart. These times together are what put the glow in my windows.

But the interaction in our house is not always gentle and serene. It's just as likely to be rambunctious and rowdy. The pillows of our large family room sofas get thrown a lot during our family gymnastics sessions. We roll on the

floor; we wrestle. The girls play "Hop on Pop," which means they sit on my chest and bounce up and down like kangaroos. (I can already see that this game will have an age limit.) These are wonderful times we have together, full of the innocence of childhood and the warmth of family togetherness. The girls love those times. Nanette and I love them, too. We love being able to tumble around on the rug together. We love feeling breathless with laughter and love.

In our house, we know each other. We talk a lot. We know where each other is ticklish. We read together from children's books or from our big family Bible. We paint together, although our styles are different. (My style is a highly romanticized form of realism; the girls are still largely in their abstract period!)

We play games in our house. Merritt is just now learning checkers, and I look forward to the day she can play a heated Monopoly match with me. We sing songs—making up in enthusiasm for what we lack in talent.

We also love to bring our friends into the warm circle of the light in our home. We let the kids run wild in the rumpus room while the grownups relax and enjoy each other's company. Sometimes we play board games.

Sometimes we all go out to dinner together or take a walk in the neighborhood. Mostly, though, we just sit and talk.

Conversation, too, is what I imagine going on behind the glowing windows in my paintings. Lively conversation—about books, about old movies, about hopes and dreams, about the many blessings God gives us. Conversation that can occupy a whole evening. Conversation where people's lives touch in a meaningful way.

That kind of conversation has almost become a lost art in our high-tech age. We became aware of this loss during a summer we spent in a little English village. There, social activity is built around the town pub. People gather there to eat a simple meal or drink the famous English ale, but mostly to talk and laugh.

ere in America, we've installed television sets everywhere so that people never have to converse. Even restaurants have given in to this trend, and it is often difficult to find a table where you can escape the distracting glare of a television set. Have you ever walked at night by a window where the television was on? The light is dim and cold. But walk at night by a window where a fire is flickering, where a candle is lit, and see the difference. The warm glow in the windows is so inviting that it draws you in.

It's not high-tech entertainment that puts the warmth in the windows, but human connection. It's human warmth that makes up the golden glow. And I think that most of us are instinctively drawn to that warmth.

And yet the glow in the windows is not reserved solely for families like mine. The warmth is not exclusive, not unreachable. The windows can shine wherever you find a resting place for your heart.

I think of my mother. She and my father parted ways when I was very young, and she has lived alone for nearly twenty years, since the day my brother and I left for college. And

Home! . . . how much it all meant to him, and the special value of some such anchorage in one's existence. . . . It was good to think he had this to come back to, this place which was all his own, these things which were so glad to see him again and could always be counted upon for the same simple welcome.

—KENNETH GRAHAME
THE WIND IN THE WILLOWS

yet her house always glows with that "someone's home" light because my mother, more than almost anyone I know, is serenely at home with herself.

Every inch of her house tells a tale of her busy and involved life. Tangled skeins of yarn bear testimony to the cat's good time, and gardening tools lean in a corner of her garage. Projects sprawl on the tables, waiting for her attention, and pencils and notebooks are everywhere, filled with her notes and observations. My mother's cozy little nest is every inch her own; to me it exudes the same welcoming glow that my own home holds.

You can put that same light in your windows by surrounding yourself with your work and your play and your memories. If you love art, cover your walls with paintings or prints that speak to your soul and bring you peace. If you love music, put the piano in the center of the room and keep the stereo tuned to your favorite station. Pad the sofa with fluffy pillows. Drape a soft afghan on your favorite chair—and put a favorite book nearby. And yes, you might want to light a candle on the windowsill.

You also put the light in your windows by sharing your life with others. Invite neighbors or friends for an evening of checkers or chamber music or conversation, giving them a taste of your life.

But most of all, you put a light in the window by coming home to yourself. By becoming friends with who you are and who you can be. By finding a resting place for your heart.

My constant prayer is that my work will inspire others with a vision of how good life can be. And time and time again, God has graciously given me evidence of the fruits of my labor. At a recent visit to a gallery I was approached by a woman whose story touched my heart.

"Mr. Kinkade?" she began hesitantly. "I just wanted to tell you what this painting did for me." The print she was pointing to showed a cozy little thatched cottage surrounded by bright, exuberant gardens. "Because I feel as though it saved my life."

Naturally enough, this dramatic statement caught my attention, and I spent the next few minutes listening to the woman's story. She told of a life broken by the pain of loss, of a hopelessness so complete that she eventually decided she couldn't go on living. But then a tiny spark of possibility was struck. While she sat in a doctor's office, she found her eyes drawn to a print on the wall—the same print she was pointing to now. And as she phrased it to me, "It was like I was wandering down the little path, smelling the flowers. And I just knew what was inside—I could see the little rocking chair, the book beside it, and it was all so peaceful. I'm saving my money for my own little place with a garden—just like the garden in the picture. Before, I never thought something like that was possible for someone like me. When I saw that painting, I got a glimpse of hope—of a world where I could be happy again."

As that woman ended her story, she told of the new life she had built for herself. "My whole world is brighter now," she concluded.

Needless to say, that conversation affected me more deeply than I can express. It reminded me of the need that people have for a bit of light and warmth in their lives—and the healing power that can come from a little spark of hope.

After all, my painting didn't save that woman's life. The painting was only a catalyst, a starting point that began the process of rekindling hope in her heart. She took it from there, nursing that little spark into a cozy fire that lit the windows of her life.

My painting started her on the homeward path. But she was the one who made the choice to leave her pain behind and come home to simpler times.

And that, in the end, is the way it always works. ❃

Home is where the heart is,

The soul's bright guiding star.

Home is where real love is,

Where our own dear ones are.

Home means someone waiting

To give a welcome smile.

Home means peace

and joy and rest

And everything worthwhile.

—Anonymous

The Voice of Creation

The Simplifying Lessons of Nature

And this our life . . .

Finds tongues in trees, books in the running brooks,

Sermons in stones, and good in everything.

—WILLIAM SHAKESPEARE

There's a little beach town not far from our home where our family loves to go for weekends. I set up my portable easel and paint in the brisk, salty air. The girls play in the sand. We all take walks on the shore. It's a great opportunity to be out of doors and to get away from it all.

But one of my favorite things to do when we're down at the beach is watch the people. I like to sit on the little patio with a cup of coffee and just enjoy the human parade on the scenic walk below.

I'm especially fascinated by all the different things people do there on the edge of the ocean, while the sun is smiling and the waves are caressing the shore.

Some walk by in twos, deeply engaged in conversation.

Some pound the sand with their running shoes as they stride along, their faces deep in athletic concentration.

Skaters weave in and out among the foot traffic on the paved path, with barely a glance at the bicyclers and the stroller pushers and the tourists with their cameras and the readers in their beach chairs. Children are everywhere, their high-pitched voices mingling with the sound of seagulls and surf.

Every once in a while, someone will come out to the beach and sit motionless on a rock. Maybe they intend to stay for just a few minutes. But those few minutes quickly become an hour, and before long they've grown entranced by the rhythms of the surf. Hour after hour, they sit patiently near the ocean, studying it and listening to its voice. They may be there until sunset, with nothing to show for their day but a sunburn and a peaceful heart.

And those are the people, I suspect, who are living in simpler times.

It's no secret that human beings can find healing and restoration through contact with nature. It's no secret that growing things soothe the mind, that wild things uplift the soul, that rocks and hills and trees do something undefinable but positive for the human spirit.

Stones and trees speak slowly

and may take a week

to get out a single sentence,

and there are few men,

unfortunately, with the

patience to wait for

an oak to finish a thought.

—GARRISON KEILLOR

*S*omething deep in our spirit makes us long to be out of doors, to be renewed in the presence of nature. If you listen, the world of sky and water and trees can teach you. It can change you. It can make your life profoundly simpler and more satisfying.

But you have to be paying attention. You have to be still. You have to listen and touch and smell. And sometimes you have to wait.

I am not by nature a quiet or reflective type. It was my pencils and paints that taught me to listen to nature rather than just visiting nature. It was my art that slowed me down enough to see and hear the stories of the natural world.

From the time I was very small, I carried a sketchbook with me when I went on a hike or a long bike ride. I loved to loll on the golden hillsides and sketch the lumpy green oak trees or the patterns of the clouds.

As I grew a little older, I took my paints outdoors as well. I began the practice of plein-air painting—which simply means painting on location, out of doors. I started with just a few brushes and a jar of turpentine and a couple of tubes of paint packed away in a satchel. Today I use a portable studio I designed myself—a lightweight box that holds my paints and canvas and folds up into an easel. I can even attach a little umbrella to protect me from sun or rain.

I can take my portable studio almost anywhere my feet can walk. I have taken it to the desert, to the mountains, to New England villages and Irish castles, to the streets of Paris and San Francisco. I've even set it up in my own backyard and painted while the children played around me and attempted a few dabs with the paints themselves.

Plein-air painting gives me an excuse to get outdoors. It gives me backgrounds and ideas for my paintings. But most important, it forces me to experience nature on its own terms. When I am painting a scene, I'm not just walking through it or skating through it or skiing down it. I am sitting still for hours at a time, soaking it in, observing the details, breathing in the air, and listening to the sounds. I am becoming a part of the natural world and letting it become a part of me.

But you don't have to be a painter to have this same experience. You can be a bird watcher. You can take a journal to a little park behind your house. You can take a walk in the woods or a drive out to a desert spring.

The point is to be quiet and receptive.

The point is to watch and listen for nature's messages.

To me, the beauty and intricacy and magnificence of the outside world has always shouted an unmistakable message that an astoundingly creative Intelligence is behind it all. As an artist, my eye is trained to recognize good work. And the work I see in a fiery fluorescent autumn tree or in craggy tumbled boulders or the subtle patchwork of color in a sun-kissed field bespeaks an imagination and a craftsmanship far beyond that of any human artist.

The loudest message the natural world speaks to me has always been a comforting, uplifting message about God and His connection with my world.

But you don't have to take my word for it.

Listen to the trees, for what they have to say to you.

Listen to the ocean, to the many-voiced stories the waves tell.

Listen to the sun, the moon, the stars, to the echoing, intimate voice of the heavens. ✾

The heavens declare

the glory of God:

the skies proclaim

the work of His hands.

Day after day

they pour forth speech:

night after night

they display knowledge.

There is no speech or language

where their voice is not heard.

Their voice goes out

into all the earth,

their words to the ends

of the world.

—THE BOOK OF PSALMS

The Unhurried Imagination

Creative Simplicity

Creativeness in the world is,

as it were,

the eighth day of creation.

— Nicolas Berdyaev

It had been a long day for Nanette. I could see it in her drooping eyes, her tired face. So as soon as baby Winsor was asleep that evening, I volunteered to take Merritt and Chandler to the studio with me for a couple of hours.

Quickly we gathered an armload of books and toys and headed next door to the studio. I secured my current work in progress on the easel and set up my palette. Merritt and Chandler snuggled up on the sofa among a gathering of toys. And then I settled down to paint while Merritt picked up her book.

For a while, Chandler listened to Merritt's story, but then she lost interest. Out of the corner of my eye I saw her slide down off the couch and drift toward the supply closet. She returned with an armful of paper, styrofoam, scissors, tape, and glue.

"I'm going to make a hat," she told me.

"Are you?" I arched my eyebrows and continued my work as she sprawled on the floor and began working.

Before I knew it, Merritt had finished her reading and joined her sister on the floor. She located her crayons and started work on a drawing that to me looked like a man being electrocuted.

"He's swimming," Merritt said. "That's the way the water looks."

"Well," I said. "I like it."

"I like it, too."

I returned to my canvas. Chandler and Merritt returned to their work, too. All was quiet except for the low-pitched drone of a jazz tune on the radio and the squeak of styrofoam as Chandler cut and twisted it to make her hat.

I looked at my canvas, where a woodland stream was just beginning to sparkle into life. Then I looked at the two girls there on the floor, their heads bent intently over their work. And suddenly, unexpectedly, I was hit by a surge of contentment, a sense that I was very close to the center of happiness in its deepest form.

What a joy it is to be able to create something. Creativity is one of the great privileges of being human.

You apply hands and mind and spirit to fashion something that did not exist before in that precise form. You touch the universe with your own unique personality and somehow at least a little corner of the universe is changed. And in the process, a part of you is created anew.

There is something deeply refreshing about any truly creative pursuit. And the benefits of creative endeavor don't depend on the quality of the endeavor. It is the very act of creating that renews you.

This is why I am so passionate about encouraging people to paint or draw—to *create*—regardless of whether or not they have "talent." I believe that any creative endeavor pays magnificent benefits for the time invested.

Not only does it afford the simple, childlike satisfaction of playing with materials—smearing

paint, scribbling ideas and images, pounding with hammer and nails—but it also helps us make connections and understand life a little better.

Creativity is woven into the fabric of simpler times. And there are as many paths to creativity as there are human beings on this planet. You can be a creative homemaker and mother. (I am married to one.) You can also be a creative builder, a creative gardener, a creative hang glider. There is creativity in solving personal problems, in overcoming obstacles, in keeping relationships warm.

Creativity is not optional equipment. It's a built-in potential, a seedling planted deep in the human personality. And like any other human possibility, creativity can be helped to grow and flourish. Because both my happiness and my livelihood depend on maintaining my own creativity, I have a vested interest in understanding it. So I have watched other people and taken note of myself, and I have reached a few conclusions.

First of all, creativity is contagious. You catch it from being around other creative people. That's what was happening with my girls that night in my studio. My girls saw me making something new, and they were irresistibly drawn to make something, too.

That happens to me all the time. My own creativity thrives when I expose myself to what others are doing. I love to wander through galleries and museums, to read art books and monographs, to let myself be uplifted and inspired and humbled. I love to be around other artists, to talk together and even to paint or sketch together.

But exposure to creativity is much more than just talking shop with people who share the same endeavor. I find that my creativity as an artist soars through exposure to many different kinds of endeavors. I love to read—everything from fine literature to pop culture. I listen to books on tape while I paint. I pore through volumes of romantic poetry, through twentieth-century adventure novels. I collect popular literature from the 1930s, 1940s, and 1950s—dime novels, pulp magazines, and advertising. I browse antique shops, go to movies, attend meetings with creative people in the company that publishes my prints. And of course I make plenty of time to get out in nature, to let myself be inspired and renewed by contact with the work of the Creator.

Creativity is contagious, but that's just the beginning of the process. Motivation needs to turn to ideas, and ideas need to be incubated. You need to move things around in your head and with your hands. You experiment. You move your mind around, allowing yourself to look at what you're doing from different angles.

One of my most helpful creative tools is an idea board in my study. On it I post notes, sketches, fragments of thoughts, ideas, verses, cartoons—whatever has stirred my imagination in recent days. And then, whenever I pass by, I look over the board and rearrange the items. Because I am a very visual person, this process seems to stir the pot of my creativity, encouraging me to think in fresh ways.

And contrary to much popular wisdom, I have found that all of this happens best in a structured environment. Creativity flourishes under a gentle routine. It delights in an unhurried atmosphere. It requires feeding and nurturing, but not constant stimulation and "enrichment." And it is not so easily stifled as some people would have you think.

Rules, for example, don't stifle creativity—at least not in themselves. Creativity can blossom within a structure, just as tomato plants thrive in their cages and roses bloom on their trellises.

Repetitive routines don't necessarily stifle creativity either. Some of my best ideas have come while I sat for hours signing my name to prints. Shelling peas, walking to the store, any kind of "mindless" physical routine can provide a valuable backdrop for the creative mind to work. In fact, I find that the simple, routine act of walking is a wonderful stimulus to creative thinking.

Up to a point, deprivation doesn't even stifle creativity. In fact, imaginations often soar in very simple or even bare environments. Some of the world's greatest art and literature has come from men and women who knew deprivation. And even people with no professional background in art have demonstrated remarkable ingenuity in constructing a life out of the materials at hand—as evidenced by patchwork quilts and cantilevered barns and carved wooden animals and other examples of frontier handiwork.

I grew up in a very simple, unembellished environment, in a small town where I often felt starved for experience. But my brother and I were always inventing mysteries, making up stories to act out, building tree forts and networks of tunnels in the high grass. And of course I had lots of time to be outside, to ride my bike, to wander around with my sketchbook and draw. My creativity was not hampered in the least by my relative lack of "enriching" activities.

To be creative, all you need is room to play, room to think, room to just be.

If you're not sure what to do next, why not get down on the floor and put together a hat? 🌿

Our creativity will become

our prayer, born of

simple attention to what

is around, and enhancing

the world by its expression.

—ELIZABETH J. CANHAM

At Work and at Play

A Simple Balance

My job is real work, and real work is play, not drudgery.

—Madeline L'Engle

No matter how old I grow, a part of me will always be Tom Sawyer.

I'll never forget the first time I read Mark Twain's famous chronicle of boyhood, because that other Tom's life felt so familiar to me. The time frame was different, but Tom Sawyer's story was the story of my young life—running free through a little town, getting into mischief, doing chores (or getting out of them), going to school, learning lessons . . . but most of all playing. Playing hard and in earnest. Building forts

and go-carts. Exploring woods and hills and old buildings. Making up games. Solving mysteries. Inventing adventures.

I'm still doing it. There is still a boy at play in my man's life, in my man's work. And I don't apologize for my Tom Sawyer streak, because I am convinced it makes me a better worker and a better human. It certainly helps me live in simpler times.

I do believe that work is important, that it's all but impossible to lead a happy and simple life without some form of meaningful work. But meaningful work is not at all the same thing as grim, nose-to-the-grindstone labor.

All meaningful work contains an element of play—and I believe we work better when we learn to play well. But our society as a whole seems to have forgotten how to play, how to simply have fun, just as we've lost track of the meaning of work and service and vocation.

We can relearn the secret of meaningful work and restorative play—of work that is fun and play that is active and purposeful. And we can start by watching children play—because play, after all, is children's work.

A group of five-year-olds is clustered on a playground. They are playing at being unicorns or superheroes. They are stalking wild game in Africa or arranging boards to build a playhouse or digging for diamonds. And this play is purposeful. It has meaning. These children may be unable to articulate what they are doing, but they know it matters, that it's important.

The purpose of children's play, of course, is learning. Through fantasy, through make-believe, through role playing, through invention, children learn how to interact with their world and with each other.

Children's play is also active rather than passive. It is wholehearted and absorbing. Whether they are involved in a game of make-believe or an impromptu soccer match or a session with paper and crayons, children throw their whole beings—mind, soul, knees, and elbows—into what they are doing. They become what they play. They take it seriously.

And yet children also enjoy the challenge of learning, trying, interacting. They laugh. They yell. The fact that play has a purpose doesn't stop it from being fun.

And I really think that's the way our work is meant to be. We were intended to find joy and even fun in meaningful work, even as we find challenge and purpose in restorative play. That's how I've always felt about my work. In fact, I often feel like the most fortunate man in the world because I make my living doing something I would do for free, something that never fails to bring me fun and challenge. I get paid to do my hobby.

Planning a painting, blocking out a scene, structuring a composition bring me the same enjoyment I used to have putting together a tree house or working a puzzle. And there is also the elemental satisfaction of playing with paint, watching the layers grow, the colors change. It's the same joy children get when they are dabbing their fingers in paint and smearing them on paper.

What a privilege to be a professional puzzle solver and fingerpainter—with the added satisfaction of sharing what I create with others.

I feel blessed to be able to make my living the way I do.

But I have to tell you: I felt the same way when I worked in a gas station.

That was during the art-student chapter in my life. The work was routine, the hours were inconvenient, the pay was miniscule. My surroundings were grimy, the clientele grumpy.

And yet I still managed to have fun at that job. I observed an endless parade of humanity who came through the doors. I made up stories about them in my head and sketched them from memory. I played games with myself to see how quickly I could make change or reset the pumps. And I took pleasure in serving, in knowing I helped people get through their day.

Attitude can make a dynamic difference. The right attitude really can help you see the grind as a game. It can help your stress level drop and your life grow simpler and more peaceful.

Every job has elements of drudgery. Every job has elements you like less than others. But I truly believe that almost any task can offer a measure of enjoyment if it is approached with the right spirit.

*E*ven my "most fortunate man in the world" profession, for instance, has elements that are not inherently fun. Sometimes I must sit and sign my name to thousands of prints at a time—a potentially mind-numbing, back-breaking chore. Sometimes I must sit through long meetings or paint into the wee hours of the morning to finish a piece on deadline. Sometimes I barely have time to unpack from one trip before it's time to head for the airport again.

And yet I have found ways to approach these less favorite tasks and circumstances with an eye to both service and fun.

When we do a signing, for instance, we try to make a celebration of it. While my colleagues stack the canvases and I sign my name for hours on end, we put on old movies, bring in Mexican food, talk and make jokes, race the clock to see how many we can do in an hour. We have a good time. And the work gets done—perhaps even faster.

Nanette and I do the same thing with my travel schedule. When we can, we try to turn business trips into family outings. I bring Nanette and the girls along, and between meetings we go out to explore. At the very least, we use the time to talk and just be together. But if my family can't come with me, I try to enjoy the time alone. In between obligations, I treat myself to an afternoon of plein-air painting or just take a walk.

Even when I can't manage to turn a routine task into a pleasant experience, I find I can make it more pleasant by casting it in a context of meaning. I try to see a request for an interview as a sign that my work is communicating with people, a trip as a sign that I am reaching my goals, a busy day as a sign that I must be doing something right.

And of course I laugh a lot.

Laughter is absolutely vital if you want to keep your work playful and your life simple. And laughter can save you when your work grows grim. Even when I can find no other benefit, I can usually manage a laugh at myself or at the absurdity of a situation I've gotten myself into.

Late at night, especially, when the deadline is pressing and my eyelids are drooping, my sense of humor is there to keep me company, to keep me from becoming too stressed. Of course, those are the hours when little details may appear in my paintings that wouldn't appear at more normal hours.

It was late at night, for instance, that a vintage World War I submarine found itself under a bridge of the River Seine, silently lurking in the shadows while busy Parisians hurried by. It was late at night when the waves of San Francisco Bay suddenly bore a little bottle with a love letter to Nanette. It was late at night when a tiny cat appeared in the window of a cottage, staring intently at a tinier mouse in another window.

In the morning, sometimes, these tiny little touches don't seem quite as amusing. But I leave them in. To me, they are part of the enjoyment I find in my work. I love the feeling of creating a puzzle for my viewers, of weaving mystery and adventure and fun even in the act of viewing a painting. I love the sense that we can all laugh together. That my joy is shared with someone else. Because I bless others, I myself am blessed.

And that really makes me feel like the most fortunate man in the world. ❋

Don't always

act your age.

Have fun on the job.

Let some of

the child

in you show.

Laugh.

— Luci Swindoll

Romancing Your Life

The Power of a Little Passion

How do I love thee?

Let me count the ways.

—Elizabeth Barrett Browning

When I'm reading our town newspaper, I often browse the want ads. These ads offer a fascinating glimpse into our culture. For example, there seems to be an increasing number of lonely people in the world, because I've noticed more and more ads placed by single people searching for a friend or mate. I've found these ads to be so revealing about people's basic yearnings and needs.

Most of the time, what seems to be missing is romance. People seem especially hungry to take moonlit walks on the beach with a special someone. They yearn for evenings by a fire. They want someone to share music with, special dinners with, unforgettable moments with.

Who could blame them? I love those things myself, and I thank God daily I have my lovely wife to share romantic moments with.

But I always find myself wondering about something when I read those "romance wanted" ads. I wonder, do these people ever actually walk on the beach themselves? Do they enjoy fine food and music, savor special moments in their lives, enjoy moonlight and starlight and rainy-day walks beneath an umbrella?

Contrary to popular opinion, romance is not a relationship—although it can add fullness and spice and excitement to a connection between two people. Romance is not hearts and flowers and violins, although an evening of hearts and flowers and strings can be soaringly romantic.

Romance is instead an attitude, a set of habits, a way of encountering the world. You are a romantic when savoring experience is a priority for you, when you are willing to invest time and energy into making your experiences more vivid and memorable.

I have long been in the habit of planning special experiences, rewarding myself with simple little pleasures that may cost little but pay high emotional dividends.

For instance, every day I plan my lunch break. I don't just say, "Well, looks like it's noon; better go grab a sandwich or just eat while I work." Instead, I look forward in anticipation to an hour in the fresh air with my lunch in my lap and a book in my hand. Or I make plans to walk to town in the bright spring sunshine, sit on a bench in the square, and watch the people.

The other day I decided to spend my lunch break shopping for a small wooden box to give as a gift. I walked downtown and wandered through several antique stores until I found my prize—a wonderful little chest of carved mahogany. Then with my package in hand I meandered down the street to my favorite little cafe and ordered a cup of coffee.

That was a simple little interlude, and yet it added a special romantic touch to my day. The enjoyment it brought me was far out of proportion to the little energy and money I invested in it.

I will make you brooches
    and toys for your delight
Of bird-song at morning
    and star-shine at night.
I will make a palace fit
    for you and me
Of green days in forests
    and blue days at sea.
—ROBERT LOUIS STEVENSON

We live in a beautiful world, one that is shimmering with romance. It's all around you, rich and lovely and exciting. It comes into your life when you open yourself to savor your moments—happy and sad, beautiful and mundane, alone or with someone you love.

Of course, there is special joy in sharing your romantic life with the person you love best in all the world.

My ongoing romance with my wife, Nanette, is one of the constant pleasures of my existence. After many years of marriage, we are countless things to one another—business colleagues, parental partners, and friends.

But we are always and forever lovers, ever seeking out new ways to keep the romantic spark in our life together. We seek out time to be alone together, even if it's just a walk through the neighborhood. We set aside a night each week for a date, dressing up for each other, lighting candles, savoring a kind of quivering formality that reminds us of the times when we were young teenagers falling in love.

Most of all, we plan surprises for each other. We orchestrate special moments, great and small, that show we have listened carefully and observed the other person's wants and needs and invested precious energy just to make each other feel loved. In a sense, the history of our relationship is the history of such planned moments.

Nanette savors memories of the anniversary on which I presented her with a framed "early Kinkade." It was a painting of a boy and a girl walking in the moonlight—a portrait of us at a very early point in our relationship. I had painted it years before, after coming home from a date with Nanette, and I had saved it. Now it hangs in a place of honor in our home.

I, in turn, remember the year when Nanette orchestrated a surprise party for my birthday. She went to incredible lengths to prepare the food and put up decorations and sneak thirty of our friends into our house without my suspecting what was going on. And she did it. I was surprised into speechlessness.

Such elaborately planned gestures are a treasured element of our romantic life. Some we even plan together, like the trip to Paris we took on our third anniversary. We couldn't afford the trip. We didn't have time to make the trip. But we went anyway, and we had the time of our lives. We came back from that experience with the firelight burning in our hearts.

But romantic moments and gestures need not be so large to be meaningful. Romance can be as simple as a love note hidden in the laundry, a soda with two straws, a shared glance over the heads of the children, a bouquet waiting with a restaurant reservation. It can be an ordinary experience shared—like sports or hiking or sketching. Sometimes, it is the small events that carry the sweetest pleasure and evoke the deepest passion.

OLDE
PORTERFIELD
TEA ROOM

JUSTIN PORTERFIELD
PROP

EST. 1735

WELCOME

TIPPERTON

CHANDLERY

52
CHANDLERY RD

In a way, romance is an affirmation and a celebration of the simplest, most important things in life. We romance our lives when we take time to look at each other, to appreciate our experiences and our loved ones, to really live our own lives. Romancing one's life is the most personal of pursuits. It will always reflect the specific interests and talents of the people involved.

When Nanette is sharing her love with me, she usually speaks in her own personal romantic language; she offers me the gift of time and energy. She loves to cook, and she knows I enjoy fine food, so she puts together romantic dinners. She is athletically inclined, and she knows I like to play golf, so she took golf lessons so we could hit the greens together. Because she shares my taste for exploration and adventure, she has strapped on many a backpack and joined me on the trail.

And of course, I try to employ my own talents to romance my wife. The habit of paying her tribute in my paintings began with a whim and has continued to add a special spark in our life together. Nanette loves it when I hide her initial in my paintings—when I carve "N"s into my painted trees and emblazon them onto the sides of buildings. She loves it when I leave little sketches and silly notes in the house for her. She loves it when I roughhouse with the children and read to them. For her, my involvement in parenting our children is romantic.

Your own romantic language will consist of whatever brings you pleasure, whatever makes you feel alive, whatever makes you feel safe and loved, whatever is most uniquely you. These are the experiences you can savor, the experiences that strengthen your connections to the people you love and to your own heart and soul.

But whether single or married, in love or alone, what does a little romance require but a little planning, a little attention, a little passion?

When it comes to romancing your life, a little goes a long, long way. ❋

Love doesn't grow

on trees like

the apples in Eden—

it's something

you have to make.

And you must use

your imagination.

—JOYCE CARY

Just Around the Bend

Cultivating a Hobo's Heart

Afoot and light-hearted I take to the open road,

Healthy, free, the world before me,

The long brown path before me leading wherever I choose.

—WALT WHITMAN

As a child, I was endlessly exploring the brown grassy hillsides and oak-dotted meadows around my hometown of Placerville. My best times came when my brother Pat and I set out on our bikes with sketchbooks and sandwiches and a dayful of endless hours in our pockets to spend as we pleased. We memorized sights and sounds. We collected experiences. We lived in the moment, with tomorrow always tantalizingly around the bend.

In those days of boyhood freedom, my heart dreamed of moving past my own familiar haunts. I longed to go further, to see more, to explore places I had never even dreamed of.

Even then, I had a hobo's heart.

For me, it's the twists and the turns and the curves and surprises that make the journey of life more meaningful and more fun. Some of life's most important lessons, its most resplendent joys, happen when you put yourself in the path of serendipity.

For me, a hobo's heart is an attitude, a set of mind. It's an insatiable curiosity, a chronic itch to discover what's out there beyond your own backyard, a breathless anticipation over what might be around the next bend of life's road.

I quickly learned that being an artist is a perfect excuse for being a hobo. An artist is by definition a collector of experience. And there's always another vista around the bend, beckoning an artist to see the world from another perspective. So it was that as I grew, my artistic ambitions kept my heart on the road—although I suspect I would have been an explorer anyway.

It was while I was a student that I started the practice of going on "hoists" with my friend James Gurney. "Hoist" was our makeshift word for a sketching adventure—an excursion with sketchpads to a mountaintop, a train yard, a small town, an inner-city neighborhood. We relished the surprise and adventure of it. We never knew where we would end up. And we filled both our sketchbooks and our memories with unforgettable people and places.

Then came the ultimate hoist, when we actually did become hobo artists, riding the rails cross-country and sketching as we went. Eventually we wrote a book about what we saw and learned, but writing a book wasn't what we set out to do. What we set out to do was explore, to see what we could see. What we set out to do was to follow our hobo's hearts.

I've been doing it ever since, even as I worked to develop my career, to establish a company, to raise a family. That's why this Christmas will find our entire family in a rented RV, tooling our way around the deserts of California. We've set aside an entire week with no agenda except painting and exploration. When we want to stop, we'll find a campground and let the children play in the pool. When we see an intriguing side road, we'll follow it. When the sunset paints the desert soft and red and casts intriguing shadows under the rocks and the Joshua trees, we'll stop and paint—or we'll just sit and watch.

When the week is over, we'll come back home to our "normal" life. Merritt will return to school. Chandler and baby Winsor will play and learn. Nanette will cook and mount canvases and care for the family, and I will paint and sign prints and do business.

But we'll already be dreaming of the next time we'll be on the road. And already we'll be wondering what the next turn in life will bring.

I am supremely blessed to be married to a woman who shares my wandering spirit. Ever since we were married, we have had the privilege of being hoboes together. Before the girls were born, we traveled the world with backpacks and sketchbooks. When our family began to grow, our luggage list did, too, but we didn't stop going on adventures. We simply packed up the girls and took them with us. I have hiked innumerable trails with a baby in a backpack and a chubby little hand holding on to mine.

It has certainly made our life incredibly richer. And it couldn't have happened if we hadn't made the commitment to living in simpler times.

One of the reasons we try to keep such a close watch on our time commitments is that we are committed to making space for serendipity. We don't want our life packed so full that we are too busy to explore or too jaded to want a surprise.

How can you go exploring when every minute is planned?

How can you have surprises when every hour is scheduled?

We leave sizable gaps in our schedule for road trips and family outings. We ration the time and energy we spend on outside commitments and after-school activities in order to lavish our time and energy on planning our next excursion.

We plan in order to experience the joy of anticipation, but a lot of our planning involves a lot of not planning. We decide where we'll go to start—to the mountains or to the desert or to Italy or to the little park five miles away. And we may decide where our home base will be—perhaps a rented RV or a campsite or a cabin or home. From there, though, we stop planning. Or rather, our plan is not to plan.

Whenever we hit the hobo road, we defer to the spirit of serendipity.

We reserve the right to travel byroads on a whim, to cancel one set of plans in favor of a completely different one, to spend an entire day in one spot instead of pushing on to where we thought we'd go. We take risks on possibilities rather than sure things.

Often, the unexpected happens. I can still see us standing by a cold Montana roadside next to a dead steer and a totaled pickup truck loaded with camping gear—Nanette four months pregnant, me wondering how we would make it back to town.

And I can see the two of us standing on a crooked little cobblestone street in Italy, staring ruefully at a broken rain gutter while a tiny old woman gave us a thorough tongue-lashing in Italian we couldn't understand. Our borrowed RV, trying to maneuver in the narrow space between overhanging roofs, had scraped the gutter and left it dangling. We had visions of spending the night in a little Italian jail.

And yet the alchemy of memory has managed to turn even these moments into golden experience.

The wreck in Montana left us unhurt and eventually led to a wonderful experience of painting in West Yellowstone with an old friend and a new friend who let us stay in his home. The incident of the broken rain gutter ended up costing about seven dollars— and it still makes us laugh. The way we look at it, we have very little to lose by putting ourselves in the path of serendipity.

If we hadn't been willing to rent an Irish cottage sight unseen, for example, we would have missed the lovely sapphire lake set in brilliant green, the simple but cozy accommodations, the ruined castles around the bend. We would never have attended the village singalong and sat rapt while children danced and grandparents told stories and the whole town joined in the singing.

If we hadn't been willing to ask questions and jump at opportunities, we would never have been able to spend two weeks painting in Norman Rockwell's old studio, looking at the world as that great painter saw it, trying to see the landscape through his eyes. Or we would have missed the lovely Chinese festival of lanterns—the whole village lit with tiny paper lanterns—which we happened upon by accident in Monterey, California.

For us, the rich dimensions such experiences give to our lives are worth any inconvenience we may encounter from not knowing ahead of time what's going to happen. They are worth the sacrifices we must make to keep our time free for travel and discovery.

And that's true for you as well, whether or not your budget or schedule allows for distant adventures. The same eye for exploration that carries you far from home can also carry you joyfully through your days closer to home.

You can take a family jaunt to the little town thirty miles away. Hang out in the local coffee shop. Poke around in that little antique shop you've driven by a dozen times on your way to someplace you've planned to go. Pack along your camera and your notebook and your sketchbook. For the cost of a tank of gas and a paper sack of sandwiches you can have an adventure to remember.

If you have a hobo's heart and a spirit of adventure, you can turn a walk through the neighborhood into an excursion. If you know a child, ask him or her for assistance. Children so often know the secret of finding wonder in the most common places.

You don't even need to go out of doors in order to go exploring. If you are willing to let your spirit wander free, an afternoon at the art museum can be an unforgettable adventure. An evening with a good book can be a trek into the unknown. An hour spent with an intriguing companion can be an adventurous journey—for what is more mysterious and full of surprise than the human soul?

Like most other aspects of simpler times, exploration and discovery and serendipity depend more on your frame of mind than on your circumstances. You will make discoveries, you will enjoy adventures, because you are willing to open your eyes and your heart to discovery and adventure.

And then, in the process, something else will happen—or at least that has been my experience.

As you set out into your world with a hobo's heart, your world will grow larger. And you will be growing, too. As you encounter challenges along your way, you will grow stronger. As you adjust your route in response to your circumstances, you will grow more flexible. As you learn to treat adversity as an adventure, you will grow more hopeful, less afraid, better equipped to cope with what life throws your way.

The habit of following the twisting road, of walking with a spirit of excited anticipation, of rolling with the punches and stepping around the rocks—all these are important skills for carrying you safely through your life.

And this, of course, is the secret—the reason life is simpler when you follow a hobo's heart.

The surprises will come, regardless. The unexpected will happen. And if you're living in anticipation, making room for the unexpected, you know the joy of the road. You will be a traveler, not a refugee. You will be moving forward, not just moving along.

And I guarantee there will be wonderful surprises waiting for you—just around the bend. ❀

So let the way wind

up the hill or down,

O'er rough or smooth,

the journey will be joy

Still seeking what I sought

when but a boy,

New friendship, high adventure,

and a crown,

My heart will keep

the courage of the quest,

And hope the road's last turn

will be the best.

— HENRY VAN DYKE

Let Your Light Shine

A Life for Today and Tomorrow

What thou lov'st well

is thy true heritage.

—EZRA POUND

I've always loved the stars.

I love to stand out on a summer's night, far away from the lights of the city, and gaze up at all those winking points of light shining through the mysterious darkness. Thinking about all the endless miles that light has traveled. Wondering . . . about today and tomorrow.

When I was a child, someone told me that you can turn on a flashlight and aim it at a star, and that

even after you turned the flashlight off the light would keep going—on and on, year after year, even century after century, until it eventually reached the star.

Now I realize that concept won't hold up to any kind of scientific verification. But that image—of a tiny light shining on across the miles and through the ages—has stayed with me. It speaks to my deep desire to lead a life that matters over the long run— one that will still have an impact after I have gone.

I don't think I'm unique in this feeling. I think it's a yearning built into every human spirit. We all want our light to keep on going somehow. We all yearn to touch the stars.

And that is yet another reason to make the decisions that keep us living in simpler times.

How will we know we've succeeded? In a sense, we won't. There's nothing you or I can do to guarantee that our name or our accomplishments will be remembered here on earth. Fashions change. Memories are fickle. Cataclysms alter the face of the earth. I have no way of knowing whether a given painting will end up in a museum or be lost in a fire.

But there are some things we all can do to shine our flashlight up to the stars.

We can work to lay a legacy, to create a heritage. We can do what we do with posterity in mind. We can carry out our vocation with an intention of giving a gift to another generation.

My desire to leave a legacy is one of the reasons I've chosen to spend my life making art. Art is made to last. Most fine artists I know expect their creations to have a life beyond the next fad or the next ad campaign—preferably beyond the next generation.

In fact, nothing makes me happier than the people who buy three prints because "we have three children, and this way we can pass them on." Nothing inspires me as an artist like the thought that I may be creating heirlooms for future generations.

I am not saying my art will live forever. I have no control over earthquakes or oxidizing paint formulas or—even more fickle—artistic taste.

And yet I can still paint with the long term in mind. I can paint with an eye to universal human themes. I can strive to remain true to what I see as timeless values.

This desire to create works that stand the test of time has determined to a large degree my choice of subjects. I paint trees and mountains and gardens. I paint old, sturdy homes and cottages with warm windows that hint at family homecomings. I paint historic cities. And in all my paintings I strive for that sense of universal human longings—for home, for nature, for fellowship, for the beautiful.

The desire for longevity as an artist also helps me resist the temptation to hurry my work along, to cut corners, to think in terms of productivity rather than quality. I always try to remember what someone once told me: "They'll forget how quickly you do it, but they'll always remember how well you do it." And so I try to give each painting its due. I am willing to put in the hours I need to put in.

And yet that same desire to live for the long term tells me that my work cannot be my ultimate priority. The things we make cannot be our most important legacy.

I put my heart and my soul into my paintings, but in the long term they are still only flat pieces of canvas with daubs of color covering them. They are only material objects, just as the Empire State Building and the pyramids and the earth itself is a material object. Even these long-lasting things are not eternal.

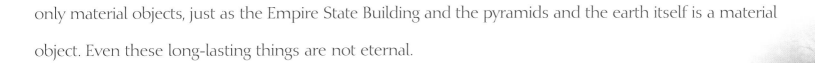My most important legacy, the one that can carry my little light onward toward the stars, will be the contribution I make to the lives of other human beings—because my faith in God affirms that human souls are the only things in this life that continue forever. Material things are subject to moth and rust and death, but according to the Bible human souls are eternal. And therefore my true heritage must be my loving contribution to other human souls.

That belief and my personal Christian faith keeps my family at the top of my list of priorities, because my family members are the human beings I touch most often and most deeply. After all, if my wife and my children are eternal beings, then the way I treat them will have eternal consequences. This, even more than my paintings, will keep my light shining and help me reach the stars.

And this principle extends even beyond my family. In giving to other humans, in serving them, in helping them, I have the opportunity to affect their eternal destiny. In service, therefore, lies my chance to touch the stars.

I've seen this reality echo and re-echo in the life of my mother, who has invested her life in the service of her fellow humans. To my brother and sister and me, she donated her energy, her care, her passion for art and literature, and her fierce determination to march to the beat of a different drummer. To the people she serves in the soup kitchen sponsored by her local church, she donates her concern and her compassion. And that, to me, is her most lasting legacy.

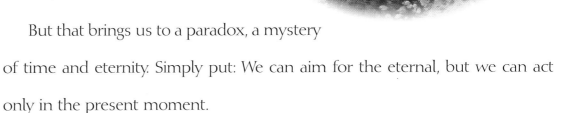

I am convinced this is true for every human being, regardless of faith, backround, occupation, or circumstance. When I am loving today, I am sending out my light to touch tomorrow's stars.

But that brings us to a paradox, a mystery of time and eternity. Simply put: We can aim for the eternal, but we can act only in the present moment.

We can work at establishing a legacy for tomorrow, but we can do this successfully only when we are living fully today. It's what I'm doing right now with my flashlight that determines whether the light will keep on going through the generations.

This reality cuts to the very heart of simpler times—the key to a full yet purposeful life. As a Christian and a man of prayer, it is what enables me to experience the present joyfully and passionately, yet still make plans for the future. It is the reality that reminds me that stopping to examine that bug with my daughters may pay longer-term dividends than rushing to my studio to finish a painting.

Our best chance of touching, in our own small way, the eternal is to live the life we're given, savoring the now, deciding for the future, remembering always that the secrets of the stars are folded tightly into the mysterious center of this present moment.

They unfold in the form of grace for where we are, purpose for where we're going, a joyous sense of enjoying the journey.

They unfold into the kind of life that's worth living.

They unfold, yesterday, today, tomorrow, into simpler times. And simpler times are eternal times. ✳

And now abide

faith, hope, love, these three;

but the greatest of these is love.

—THE APOSTLE PAUL

Glory be to God for dappled things –

For skies of couple-colour as a brinded cow;

For rose-moles all in stipple upon trout that swim:

Fresh-firecoal chestnut falls; finches' wings;

Landscape plotted and pieced – fold, fallow, and plough;

And all trades, their gear and tackle and trim.

All things counter, original, spare, strange;

Whatever is fickle, freckled (who knows how?)

With swift, slow; sweet, sour; adazzle, dim;

He fathers-forth whose beauty is past change:

Praise him.

— GERARD MANLEY HOPKINS

Paintings